Founder's Poc[...]
Founder Equ[...]

1x1MEDIA

Simple, quick answers, all in one place.

By

Stephen R. Poland

1x1 Media
Leicester, NC 28748
United States

Care has been taken to verify the accuracy of information in this book. However, the authors and publisher cannot accept responsibility for consequences from application of the information in this book, and makes no warranty, expressed or implied, with respect to its content.

Trademarks: Some of the product names and company names included in this book have been used for identification purposes only and may be trademarks or registered trade names of their respective manufacturers and sellers. The author and publisher disclaim any affiliation, association, or connection with, or sponsorship or endorsement by, such owners.

ISBN 978-1-938162-09-1

©2016 by 1x1 Media, LLC

email: info@1x1media.com

website : www.1x1media.com

Table of Contents

Table of Contents

Founder's Pocket Guide: Founder Equity Splits

What the Founder's Pocket Guide Series Delivers

We developed the *Founder's Pocket Guide* series to provide quick answers to common questions encountered by entrepreneurs. Consider the following dilemmas a founder might face:

> "I sort of know **what startup equity is**, but really don't understand the details, and I have an investor interested in my company. Where do I start?"

> "My co-founder said we need to **build a cap table to track our equity ownership**—how do we get started?"

> "My co-founders and I need to determine **how to divide the ownership** of our startup, but how can we be certain we get it right?"

> "I've heard that **convertible debt is a good funding structure for early-stage startups**. What is convertible debt and how do I approach potential investors with a funding pitch?"

The *Founder's Pocket Guide* series addresses each of the topics in a concise and easy to reference format.

Look for these current titles at www.1x1media.com:

- *Founder's Pocket Guide: Startup Valuation*
- *Founder's Pocket Guide: Cap Tables*
- *Founder's Pocket Guide: Convertible Debt*
- *Founder's Pocket Guide: Terms Sheets and Preferred Shares*
- *Founder's Pocket Guide: Friends & Family Funding*
- *Startup Crash Course: Angel Funding*

Disclaimers

The content in this guide is not intended as legal, financial, or tax advice and cannot be relied upon for any purpose without the services of a qualified professional. With that disclaimer in mind, here's our position on how to best use the guidance provided in this work.

Great entrepreneurs use all the resources available to them, making the best decisions they can to mitigate risk and yet move ahead with the most important tasks in their roadmaps. This process includes consulting lawyers, CPAs, and other professionals with deep domain knowledge when necessary.

Great entrepreneurs also balance a strong do-it-yourself drive with the understanding that the whole team creates great innovations and succeeds in bringing great products to the world. Along those lines, here's a simple plan for the scrappy early-stage founder who can't afford to hire a startup lawyer or CPA to handle all of the tasks needed to close a funding deal or form the startup:

> **1. Educate yourself on what's needed.** Learn about startup equity structures and issues, legal agreements, financing structures, and other company formation best practices, and then;

> **2. Get your lawyer involved**. Once you thoroughly understand the moving parts and have completed some of the work to the best of your ability, pay your startup-experienced lawyer or other professional to advise you and finalize the legal contracts.

With this self-educating and money-saving sequence in mind, let's dig in to this *Founder's Pocket Guide*.

In This Pocket Guide

Equity ownership affects the culture and sense of wellbeing of a startup. Founders typically sacrifice a great deal of other life opportunities to work on a startup effort. In exchange for that sacrifice, a founder wants to feel the ownership equation with any co-founders is fair.

This guide provides a framework and process to help new startup founders navigate the equity split decision process and arrive at a decision that feels fair and objective.

The following sections found later in this *Founder's Pocket Guide* highlight the equity split process:

Deciding Who the Founders Really Are

The "Take The Founder Test" section helps you take an honest look at each person's role in the startup. Does everyone involved really qualify for founder status, or are some individuals really contractors, advisors, or early employees? Founder status should not be taken lightly. Nailing down who the founders really are is the essential first step in dividing up the equity ownership of your new venture.

Reviewing Equity Split Methods

In the "Equity Split Methods" section, the text explores several factors that might justify equal equity splits and then moves on to explaining the Equity Split Scorecard methodology to help calculate unequal equity split amounts.

Using Vesting Schedules

The section called "Vesting: Earning Your Piece of the Pie" explains why establishing vesting schedules for each founder is critical. The section presents commonly used founder vesting schedules and shows how to use milestone-based vesting to solve the part-time founder dilemma.

Answering Common Equity Split Questions

Your journey of reviewing the best practices for dividing equity among multiple founders concludes with the "Common Equity Split Questions" section. This part of the book presents solutions to many additional questions that come up in connection to equity ownership among founders, including:

- If one founder is more experienced, does that warrant more equity?
- What if a founder is able to bring more money to the startup? Should she get more equity?
- Does the founder with the core idea for the startup get more equity?

Documenting Your Equity Split Decision

To wrap up this *Founder's Pocket Guide*, the "Putting Your Equity Agreement In Writing" section provides a simple example of how to document your equity split decision with your co-founders.

What This Guide Does Not Cover

Note that this guide **does not go into how to use equity to attract employees or using equity to pay service providers, advisors, development companies, or other contractors.** This guide focuses solely on the best practices of deciding the equity ownership split between the founders of a startup venture. Paying service providers or other contributors with equity is extremely problematic, with issues of vesting, stock valuation, and taxes, to name a few. It can be and is often done, however. If you want to do this, work with a very experienced startup lawyer to help you devise a stock option plan to support this use of equity.

Founder Pro Tips

 To further help guide you through the ins and outs of deciding founder equity ownership, you'll find useful Pro Tips that provide deeper insights, insider tips, and additional explanations throughout this guide.

Get The Equity Split Workbook File

Be sure to download the Equity Split Workbook (Excel) file to follow along with key examples reviewed in this guide. With a live version of the Excel file, you'll be able to test the equity split frameworks and save the outcomes to review with your co-founders. The free file includes the following components:

1. The Founder Test

2. The Equity Split Scorecard (composed of two tabs 2a. Rate Yourself, and 2b. The Equity Split Scorecard)

Grab the file here: (Note that the link is shortened using Google's URL shortening tool)

http://goo.gl/XhRTHM

Founder Equity Splits

Establishing the equity split between multiple founders is an opportunity to get some important stuff out in the open. Considering what each founder brings to the table using transparent, logical checklists and scoring methods will arrive at a split that everyone understands and finds agreeable, heading off potential disagreements down the road. Let's review some basic terms and concepts before digging in to the nuts and bolts.

Founder Equity 101

For a founder, ownership in the company is the reward for taking big risks and building the startup into a self-sustaining business. Founders earn their equity ownership by taking the highest amount of risk and giving their sustained long-term effort.

Dividing the equity ownership between multiple founders is the first step in setting the stage for a great working relationship. The equity split affects how each founder views his or her commitment and potential reward from the startup success.

Founders work for equity, not a paycheck

Most startups are very cash poor and can't provide the founders a paycheck during early days of the venture. Instead, the founders' compensation comes in the form of owning a potentially valuable venture. Later, when the startup starts making consistent profits or raises investment capital, the founders will begin to pay themselves modest salaries. And perhaps some day, the startup venture becomes valuable to a larger company and the founders may choose to sell the startup (exit), hopefully realizing a big payday. The more equity each founder owns, the larger his or her share of the exit proceeds.

Building Company Value with a View to an Exit

For example, consider a simplified exit scenario. The large and well-known MegaCorp is acquiring the small startup, StartupCo. com, founded by co-founder Bob and co-founder Jill.

Founder Bob owns 25% of the company, Founder Jill owns 25%, the employees own 20% collectively, and a few investors own the remaining 30% of the company. If the startup sells for $20 million to MegaCorp, then Bob gets .25 x $20 million = $5 million, Jill gets the same, the employees split $4 million (.20 x $20 million), and the investors get $6 million (.30 x $20 million).

Bob and Jill have been working for seven years to build the company to this level and have not taken much of a paycheck. Bob and Jill decided to split the equity 50/50 when they founded the startup, and now they can reap the rewards for the long years of low pay and hard work. They also have given up some equity ownership to investors and employees along the way.

Founders give up equity to raise funding and to attract talented employees

Early employees of the startup are often next in line for a cut of equity ownership in the startup. As part of their compensation plan, early startup employees often receive small amounts of equity in the form of stock options. The stock options become more valuable as the startup grows. If the startup gets acquired, the employees can share in the proceeds.

If the startup decides to raise equity funding from investors including angels or VCs, those investors come next in line to get a cut of the exit equity pie. Investors trade cash in exchange for an ownership stake in the venture, with the hope of getting a large return years down the road. As outside investors buy into the startup, founders give up a portion of their equity to the investors. Founder dilution is the tradeoff for getting the much needed cash to growth the venture.

The graphic below shows an example progression of declining founder ownership percentages and increasing valuation as the startup matures and raises more outside equity investment.

While the founder ownership percentage is getting diluted at each funding event, the overall valuation of the startup is increasing; therefore, the founder's portion of ownership is worth more.

Valuation and Founder Equity

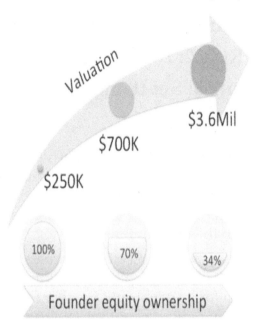

The value of the startup grows when the riskiness of the startup lowers

As the startup makes progress, launches its products, adds new customers, and streamlines supporting operations, it is reducing the risk associated with the startup surviving and ultimately succeeding. This risk reduction adds value to the startup, and at each round of equity funding, that value should be growing.

With these principals of founder equity in mind, let's move on and have a look at some more concrete rules for making equity split decisions.

Three Rules for Founder Equity Decisions

Supplementing many years of guiding startup founders in equity split discussions with research on equity split best practices, we've developed three guiding "rules" for founders to follow when talking about equity splits. Here they are:

Rule 1: Fairness above All Else
Rule 2: Everybody Vests
Rule 3: Set It and Forget It

Rule 1: Fairness above All Else

When it comes to the ownership of your startup, you always want to be certain that the equity structure of the startup is fair to all the founders. Many challenges occur while building a new company. When things get hard, you don't want lingering feelings of unfairness adding to the difficult times.

Equal is Fair. Equal ownership meets the fairness requirement, and that's why the section on equity split methods covers equal splits first. While the math for an equal split is super easy, you want to be sure you have been thoughtful about selecting an equal split. You don't want to choose an equal split just because it was the path of least resistance.

Un-equal may also be fair. Alternately, if meeting the fairness requirement means that founders decide to divide the equity of the startup **unequally**, then there should be very clear reasons for the imbalance. It's a choice you'll have to live with for the life of the startup.

Rule 2: Everybody Vests

Once founders determine the relative amount of equity each will receive, the vesting process provides a mechanism for founders to "earn" their stock shares and to answer a few common startup questions.

With written vesting schedules, founders don't own their stock shares until certain things happen—time passes, to-do items get completed, and so on.

Vesting solves many potential problems. For example, vesting helps ensure that a founder can't leave the startup effort after three weeks and still own 50% of company.

The section titled "Vesting: Earning Your Share" reviews founder vesting in detail.

Rule 3: Set It and Forget It

In other words, come to an agreement, put it in writing, and get on with building your startup. After you meet the first rule and everybody feels the split decision is fair, and you then create appropriate written vesting schedules for each founder, it's time to move on to the hard (and fun) work of building your product and finding users or customers. You do not revisit the question of who owns how much of the company.

You don't want to have to constantly re-evaluate who is getting more or less of the company. Yes, you need to spend some time tracking and documenting founder vesting as time and milestones progress, but you should not constantly monkey with the ownership balance of the company.

With these rules in mind, let's next look at some of the triggers that signal it's time to tackle the equity split topic.

When You Need To Decide

First and foremost, startup founders need to make sure the company has a product or service that customers really want, as early as possible. With this idea in mind, many founders are tempted to put off all the tedious business housekeeping tasks until later.

Worrying about equity agreements, bookkeeping systems, and other housekeeping details may seem like a misplaced effort. It's not. Don't wait to make the equity ownership decision. **Decide early,** and then get back to validating your idea and market.

With that nudging done, there are a number of events or milestones that signal the need to have the equity split meeting and make the final ownership decisions. Schedule the meeting and make the decisions:

- **After you've agreed on who the founders really are.** For many startups, this is a no-brainer; it's obvious who the founders are. Two or three friends, classmates, or co-workers have decided to make a go of their startup idea and begin taking steps to bring their vision to the world. For others, naming the founders is not so clear. To help clear up any founder ambiguity, see the section "The Founder Test" later in this guide.

- **When adding a new co-founder.** If you are adding a new person with founder status to your startup team, you must revisit the equity ownership discussion. The existing founders need to decide how much of their equity they will give up to the new co-founder. The equity split methods reviewed later in this guide offer a structure to help make these decisions.

- **When formalizing your incorporation details with your startup lawyer.** With this step, you obviously need to decide who owns how much of the company. The Articles of Incorporation, Operating Agreement (for a LLC) or the Corporate Bylaws (for a C-Corp) and various Shareholder Agreements all play a part in documenting who the owners of the corporate entity are, as well as other ground rules for the governance of the corporation, such as naming the board of directors, and outlining corporate meeting requirements.

- **Before an outside investor enters the picture.** Early stage investors are usually friends and family investors, such as a parent or sibling, or possibly an experienced startup investor such as an angel investor or angel investor group. Before you can decide how much equity to trade for the investor's cash, you need an agreement on how much each founder owns. At the end of the investment process, each founder will give up some percentage of his or her equity to the investor.

- **Before you quit your day job.** If you are at the stage when you are going to quit your day job to dedicate all of your time to the startup, it's also time to finalize your equity split agreement with your co-founders.

- **Before you hire employees.** If you are at the stage of hiring your first employees, then it's also time to clean up your startup housekeeping and decide how the equity of the company is divided among the founders. In many startups, the founders choose to create a stock incentive plan to offer new employees. Using stock options to add to, or offset, cash compensation gives employees an added incentive to work hard and stay with the company. Stock options are a form of equity ownership in the company, and founders give up some their equity to create the stock option pool. It follows that if you are deciding on the size of a stock option pool, then you must also decide how much equity the founders own beforehand.

Pro Tip

Ownership Verses Control

Many founders worry about losing voting control in their company. If all the founders' collective ownership stake in the company drops below 51% (due to giving up equity to investors and others), they fear they will lose control of the company.

To remedy this concern, some founders choose to structure the common stock of the company into two classes—Class A shares that have "super" voting power (10:1) for the founders, and Class B shares with normal (1:1) voting power for employees and other common stock stakeholders. With 10:1 voting leverage, the founders can out vote other stakeholders even if the founders' ownership percentage is less than 51%.

If you think your startup requires special Class A or "founders shares," be sure to work with your startup lawyer to review the pros an cons of a two-class common stock setup, and execute all the associated legal agreements.

The Process For Deciding Equity Splits

The next four sections of this guide outline a process to arrive at a fair and objective equity split solution for your startup. Here are the highlights of the process.

1. **Take The Founder Test.** Before you can decide on the equity ownership split of the startup, you first need to spend some time to make sure everybody involved the equity split discussion is really a founder. **This is a critical step because it solves several problems associated with startup equity.** The section called "The Founder Test" provides a framework to test everybody's founder status.

2. **Decide on the Equity Split.** With the number of true founders decided, you can next move through the process of deciding the percentage of the company each founder will own. Whether you choose to split the equity equally (50/50 for example) or allocate more equity to some founders than others (see the section called "Equity Split Methods"), be sure to stay focused on the first rule of equity splits— **fairness first.**

3. **Create Founder Vesting Schedules.** Once you've reached an equity split agreement with your co-founders, it's time to follow the second equity split rule—**everybody vests.** (See the section "Vesting: Earning Your Piece of the Pie.") Creating a vesting schedule for each founder puts a structure in place that solves many common startup problems, including offering incentives to make it over rough patches, managing equity if a founder leaves, or accounting for work done before the startup formed.

4 **Answer Any Lingering Questions.** If you need to tackle questions such as whether or how to trade equity for services, see the section "Common Equity Split Questions."

5. **Put It In Writing.** Finally, with the equity split decided and vesting schedules agree to, the last step is to document your choices. The final section of this guide, "Putting Your Equity Agreement In Writing," reviews the options for documenting your decisions.

Percentages First

When working through the equity discussions with your co-founders and advisors, it's best to think and discuss in percentages first. Bob gets 50%, Steve gets 50%, and so on. Don't worry about the number stock shares each founder will get. The details of stock shares will come later when working with your startup lawyer to formalize your corporation legal documents.

2

The Founder Test

The first step in deciding how to split the equity of your startup is to determine who the founders are.

Naming who the founders are in your startup venture might seem like an easy task. For two (or maybe three) co-workers or classmates who decide to launch a startup, it might be easy to agree that they are all the founders. The members of the founding group feel they have the skills and experience to accomplish the tasks needed to bring a new product or service to a well-defined customer and sizable market. They have the right combination of business, customer, and technical skills to either do the key tasks themselves or hire contractors to do some of the work when needed. In a case like this, there is no question about who are the founders.

In other circumstances the founder list might not be so clear. Consider the following scenario.

Let's look at an example where five people emerge from a successful Startup Weekend. (Startup Weekend is a program created and held by Techstars.) They spent the weekend building a pitch around a new business idea and won the pitch competition. They received such good feedback that they have decided to launch their product to the world and build a company around the new innovation.

Three big questions quickly come up:

1. Is everybody from the five-person pitch team really a founder?

2. Should each participant be entitled to founder status if the want it?

3. How much equity should each player get?

Some founder-wannabes might not be realistic about their ability to dedicate time and money to a startup. Many prospective founders have day jobs, families that depend on steady paychecks, or many other inflexible life obligations. While these team members might want to be part of the startup, they realistically can't make the commitment needed to make the cut of "founder."

The Founder Test developed by 1x1 Media helps you examine several factors that make up the founder role and test the commitment levels needed to bring a startup to life. In the best of outcomes for the example team mentioned above, after taking The Founder Test, everybody at the table would be realistically deserving of founder status. But that might not always be the case.

To get started, let's take a look at the factors that define the typical startup founder.

Business Team or Entourage?

It's very common for circles of close friends to end up talking about startup ideas and plans. It's fun to dream about what might be and valuable to get feedback on your ideas.

When it's time to move beyond the idea stage and choose who is really on the founding team, ask yourself this question: "Is everybody as willing and capable to do the heavy lifting required to get the startup off the ground?" You must be confident that no one on the founding team is just being allowed to "come along for the ride because they are a friend and were there from the start." Dividing the equity of your startup company is a serious matter, not a time to throw a bone to a friend, family member, or other connection just because they are part of your circle.

Key Elements of The Founder Test

What factors make you a founder? To test for founder status, you need to measure potential founders in several key categories, scoring them as either a Yes or No, and sometimes Maybe.

The Founder Test considers the following key categories:

- **Agreement** – Do the other founders think you are a founder?
- **Relationship** – Do you have a pre-existing relationship with at least one of the other founders?
- **Part-Time/Full-Time** – If you can only work on the startup part-time, do you have a plan to join it full-time soon?
- **Sacrifice** – Are you prepared to forego other life opportunities in favor of the goals of the startup?
- **Personal Runway** – Do you expect or need to be paid by the startup from the beginning?

- **Skills/Experience Fit** – Do the skills and experience of each founder fit with the needs of the startup? Technical, Business, Financial, Industry, Market Segment, etc.

You can be confident that anyone who scores well on these factors deserves a piece of the equity pie.

Let's look at each factor in more depth.

Agreement

Do the other founders agree that YOU are indeed a founder?

If there is doubt whether one of the potential founding team is really a founder, then now is the time to sort out the concerns. It's critical that you uncover uncertainties early. Talk openly about any doubts. It's better to have the team blow up now than wait until customers, employees, and investors are depending on the startup.

Relationship

Do you and your co-founders have a previous relationship? Are you co-workers, friends, classmates, or siblings? Known compatibility among co-founders is a huge influencer on startup success. Compatibility factors include your ability to work together, navigate uncertain paths, resolve conflicting opinions, and even tolerate those quirks that make us human.

Even better, if you and your co-founder(s) have worked on other projects together and brought new things to the world, you have already paved the way for the larger commitment of building a startup together.

If you don't have any previous relationship with your co-founders (you've just met), you increase the potential for poor founder team chemistry. Allocating a piece of the equity pie to someone you don't know very well is a risky proposition. That said, a previous relationship is not always a make or break factor. If all the other factors in The Founder Test align, consider using a probation period for all founders to get to know each other before deciding an equity split.

Part-Time/Full-Time

If you are only able to work on the startup effort part time, have you and your co-founders created a plan for you to join full time? To truly be considered a founder, you should be able to commit your full-time effort at some point in the near future.

See the section "The Part-Time Founder" for more details of a part-time to full-time transition plan.

Sacrifice

Founders are willing and able to give up other opportunities in favor of working on the startup effort. They are motivated by the singular goal of building the venture and ignore other distractions or opportunities that could cause them to stop working on the startup.

Also, founders organize their life commitments so they can sustain a high level of effort toward the startup's goals. Founders typically occupy a long-term role in the startup.

Founders are obligated to the other stakeholders in the business—employees, customers, investors, suppliers, the entire ecosystem that the startup inhabits.

It's important to note that sacrifice does not always mean each founder must be working full-time on the startup effort. It's very common for some founders to be in the position to work in the startup full-time, while one of more of the co-founders maintains a day jobs and works on the startup effort part-time. Be sure to see the section "The Part-Time Founder" for more details about equity split discussion in situations involving co-founders working both full-time and part-time.

Personal Runway

Do you expect or need to be paid by the startup from the beginning? Or, can maintain your current lifestyle without taking a paycheck from the startup for many months or even a few years. Even the most rapidly developing startups take 12 to 18 months to reach stable revenue, build out a team, and generate enough cash flow to pay founders modest salaries.

If you need to be paid by the startup from the beginning, you are not taking the same risk as your co-founders, assuming they are able to forego pay until later in the startup's life.

Skills and Experience Fit

The last factor to consider in The Founder Test is each co-founder's set of skills and experience, and how well those skills fit those of others on the founder team. The skills and experience factor helps answer questions like:

- Does each person on the prospective team have a clear role to play in the startup?
- Are there significant redundancies in the team?
- Are there dead weight founders, such as an "idea guy" with no other expertise?
- Are there significant gaps in your team, such as missing a technical lead?

To increase the focus on the issue of founder skills and experience, let's take a look at two scenarios—the unbalanced founding team and the balanced founding team.

The Unbalanced Founding Team

Consider a new startup team working to build a Software as a Service (Saas) business. The founding team looks like this:

- **Founder Jill.** Jill has significant technical experience. She has worked at several companies in software development roles. She has both designed and coded new commercial products and managed technical teams to build notable software products.
- **Founder Bob.** Bob has business development experience working in both startups and larger corporations. He has skills in finance, fundraising, and customer development.
- **Founder Steve.** Steve's core skills are in project management and some freelance work in graphic design. The idea for the startup came from Steve's direct project management experience working in the financial services industry.

This graphic shows how the three founders stack up in terms of their skills and experience.

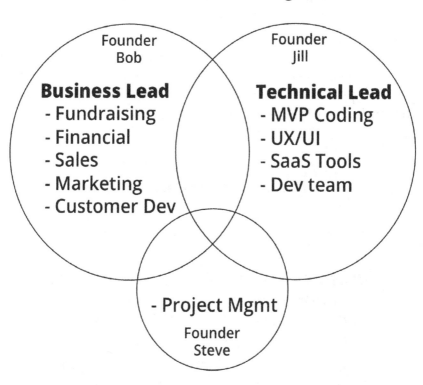

The Unbalanced Founding Team

Founder Bob

Founder Jill

Business Lead
- Fundraising
- Financial
- Sales
- Marketing
- Customer Dev

Technical Lead
- MVP Coding
- UX/UI
- SaaS Tools
- Dev team

- Project Mgmt

Founder Steve

As you can see, while Founder Steve has some project management skills, he lacks other much needed skills, creating a very unbalanced startup team.

While you could choose to allocate a much smaller amount of equity to Steve to match his inexperience, the team would likely need to recruit another founder to cover the gaps left in the team.

In this case, it is quite possible that Steve does not have the skills needed to warrant founder status.

Yes, it's a difficult conversation to "dis-invite" a potential founder from the startup team, but it's much better to tackle these difficult decisions early in the life of the startup, BEFORE any equity is allocated to the founders.

The Balanced Founding Team

In contrast to the unbalanced founding team, consider the following graphic. Here, we replace Founder Steve with a much more experienced Founder Joe. Unlike Steve's limited skill set, Founder Joe has significant domain expertise, having worked for years in the credit card processing industry (the market target for their SaaS product). This domain expertise enables the team to approach potential customers as well as establish partnerships with other industry players—a much-needed skill set for the founding team.

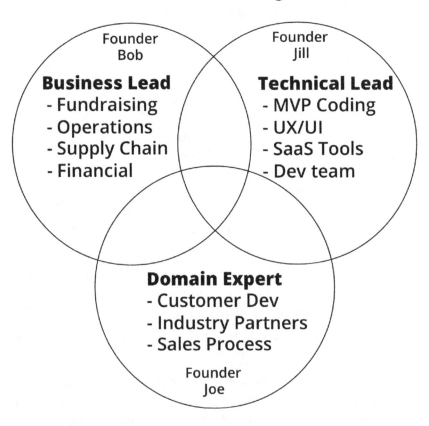

The Balanced Founding Team

Founder
Bob

Business Lead
- Fundraising
- Operations
- Supply Chain
- Financial

Founder
Jill

Technical Lead
- MVP Coding
- UX/UI
- SaaS Tools
- Dev team

Domain Expert
- Customer Dev
- Industry Partners
- Sales Process

Founder
Joe

With the startup team well balanced, the founders can move ahead with high confidence that their equity split decision will be fair and objective.

Take The Founder Test

With these critical founder attributes in mind, it's time for all founders-to-be to take the test. These steps outline the process.

1. *Each potential founder herself/himself on the test.* For each founder, make a copy of the first tab, 1. The Founder Test, in the Equity Split Workbook Excel workbook file. Each founder should then review the details of each factor of the test and score him or herself a Yes, No, or Maybe. (To mark the score in a cell, click the cell, click the drop-down list arrow that appears, then click either the check mark or blank options.)

2. *Move Maybe items to Yes or No.* Once each founder has scored his/herself, the team should come together and take a second look at the Maybe check boxes on each founder's scorecard. It may take a simple discussion to move a Maybe item to the Yes column. Or, after talking it over with your co-founders, you might decide to move a Maybe to the No column.

3. *Review and discuss all No answers.* All No items should be dis cussed with all founders present. For example, if Founder Bob answered No to the question of part-time/full-time commitment, perhaps he is not a good fit for the startup team.

4. *Have the hard discussion.* If this is a reality check for the low-scoring, on-the-bubble founder, then accept the situation. The on-the-bubble founder might be able to play a lead role in the startup at a later time. For example, if a steady paycheck is keeping a potential founder from being able to commit, that person can join the startup effort as an early employee (with stock options perhaps) once the company has the cash to pay employee salaries.

The following graphic shows an example founder test. (The Founder Test is included in the free Equity Split workbook file here: http://goo.gl/XhRTHM)

The Founder Test		Yes	Maybe	No
1. Agreement	Do the other founders think you are a founder?	✔		
2. Relationship	Do you have a pre-existing relationship with at least one of the other founders?	✔		
3. Part-Time/Full-Time	If you can only work on the startup part-time, do you have a plan to join it full-time soon?	✔		
4. Sacrifice	Are you prepared to forego other life opportunities in favor of the goals of the startup?	✔		
5. Personal Runway	Do you expect or need to be paid by the startup from the beginning?		✔	
6. Skills/Experience Fit	Do your skills and experience base fit well with those of your co-founders?		✔	

Founders that pass The Founder Test can feel confident that everybody at the equity split discussion is deserving of a piece of the ownership pie.

With all the true founders sorted out, it's time to decide how to split the equity ownership of the startup.

3

Equity Split Methods

So far, we have established *when* you need to decide on equity splits, and reviewed some thinking around *who* is really considered a founder of the startup.

Next up, the following sections review *how* to arrive at a fair equity split between you and your co-founders.

In Defense of Equal Equity Splits

This section considers the case for splitting startup ownership in equal parts. Let's start by addressing a very common startup myth.

The Myth that Equal Is Bad

Many startup advisors urge new startup founders, "Don't split your equity into equal parts."

They base the thought on the fact that founder skill sets are almost never equal; therefore you should not split the equity equally. Why this thinking is misguided?

Shouldn't the founder with more skills and experience should get more of the pie?

In reality, **only very significant differences in skill sets will move the success needle.** In most cases, the skill sets and experience of co-founders will be different, but adjusting the equity split based on minor differences in skills sets the stage for conflict among founders.

Here's the takeaway:

A trustworthy, low-conflict relationship among founders is more important than a "super optimized" initial ownership structure.

In other words, it's OK to split your equity equally. In fact, most startup founders choose this option, not only because it's easy, but also because it is fair in the majority of cases.

See the section "The Equity Split Scorecard" to learn about a framework that accounts for **significant** differences in skill and experience, resulting in a thoughtful and objective unequal equity split.

You don't need this guide to tell you how to divide by two, three, or four to get to an equal equity split. But what we hope to do in this section is to offer insights for when it's best to consider splitting your startup ownership into equal parts for each founder. In contrast, "The Equity Split Scorecard" section offers a framework for identifying why you might instead think about unequal splits, giving some more equity than the others.

Factors Supporting an Equal Equity Split

Does your team meet the criteria for splitting equity equally between the founders? If you and your co-founders can answer yes to the following factors, an equal split is a good option.

Factor #1: All founders are inexperienced. If all founders have little or no previous startup experience, dividing the equity evenly is an acceptable solution.

Inexperienced founding teams can be very successful. Each founder takes on tasks and challenges in his or her area of expertise (technical, business, design, and so on), knocking tasks off the to-do list, ultimately releasing the startup's product to the world. With everybody on the same level—learning the startup ropes for the first time—there is little justification to allocate more equity to one founder over the others.

Factor #2. No single founder is likely to dramatically increase the chances of success of the new venture more than the other founders. Stated another way, this means that each founder is at the same level of experience. If nobody on the founding team has exceptional skills and experience that will accelerate the startup or bring in paying customers, then an equal equity split is a good solution.

For example, consider a new startup team of three founders—two startup novices and a seasoned entrepreneur with previous exits under her belt. The seasoned founder probably should get more equity. She has been there before and her experience dramatically increases the odds of the startup achieving success. In this case, equal equity splits might not be the best solution.

If after considering the experience level of your founding team you decide to divide the equity ownership into equal parts for each co-founder, then it's time to build vesting schedules for each founder. If you are unsure about an equal split, move on to the "Equity Split Scorecard" section, next, to dig deeper into the skills and experience of each founder.

Unequal Equity Splits: Using The Equity Split Scorecard

Developed by the team at 1x1 Media, The Equity Split Scorecard helps founders choose equity splits that are fair and objective. The Equity Split Scorecard provides a framework for considering an unequal equity split, which means giving deserving founders more equity for very specific reasons.

The foundation of the Scorecard process is based on the idea that a founder with *exceptional expertise* in a key startup area, such as fundraising or previous exits, can substantially reduce the risk in a startup. Therefore, this founder with exceptional expertise is deserving of more equity.

For example, Founder Bob has built two prior startups and sold one to MegaCorp for a handsome return. Now Bob, Steve, and Jill are forming their new startup. Steve and Jill are startup novices. It makes sense for Bob to get a bit more equity ownership.

His experience is likely to help the new startup succeed. Steve and Jill are willing to take smaller equity positions in exchange for the opportunity to work with Bob. The Equity Split Scorecard provides a structure to quantify Founder Bob's exceptional experience and allocate more equity accordingly.

The following figure shows an example Equity Split Scorecard. We'll walk through exactly how to use the Scorecard next.

The Equity Split Scorecard					
Bonus Equity Percentage:	25%				
Founder Name:	Bob	Steve	Jill		
Everybody Starts Equal:	33.33%	33.33%	33.33%		100%
Equity Less the Bonus Pool:	25.00%	25.00%	25.00%	0.00%	
Gold Star Score					
Startup Success Factors	Bob	Steve	Jill		
1. Startup Leadership Experience	1	0	0	0	
2. Previous Exit Expertise	1	0	0	0	
3. Domain Expertise	0	0	0	0	
4. Technical Expertise	0	0	1	0	
5. Financial Expertise	0	0	0	0	
6. Customer Development Expertise	0	0	0	0	
7. Sales Expertise	0	0	0	0	
8. Marketing Expertise	0	0	0	0	
9. Fundraising Expertise	0	0	0	0	
Other					
Other					
Other					
Other					
Total Gold Stars	2	0	1	0	3
Resulting Bonus Equity %	67%	0%	33%	0%	100%
Amount of Bonus Equity Earned:	16.7%	0.0%	8.3%	0.0%	
Final Equity Split:	41.67%	25.00%	33.33%	0.00%	100%

Note that The Equity Split Scorecard does not account for common equity allocation questions such as:

- Whose idea is it?
- Who is bringing money into the startup?
- Does any work completed prior to the startup need to be taken into account?

See the later section called "Common Equity Split Questions" to learn more about how to account for each of these situations.

Startup Success Factors

At the core of The Equity Split Scorecard methodology are nine (9) startup success factors. A founder with exceptional skills and experience in these success factors will be able to move the startup ahead much faster than an average founder.

1. Startup Leadership Experience
2. Previous Exit Experience
3. Domain Expertise
4. Technical Expertise
5. Financial Expertise
6. Customer Development Expertise
7. Sales Expertise
8. Marketing Expertise
9. Fundraising Expertise

Using the **2a. Rate Yourself** tab in the scorecard, each founder scores him- or herself on these success factors and then all the founders will come together to discuss how they scored themselves. Next, they enter their scores into tab **2b. The Equity Split Scorecard.** The formulas in The Equity Split Scorecard calculate how to divide up an equity bonus pool, giving high scoring founders more percentage points of equity.

The following sections review the nine success factors in more depth.

1. Startup Leadership Experience

A founder with significant startup leadership experience has not just worked for a startup, but was a part of the founding team of a startup that reached notable milestones. A founder with exceptional experience in a leadership role is much more likely to be able to help a new startup through choppy waters. Examples include experience with:

- Building out a startup team
- Recruiting and working with a Board of Directors (BOD)
- Recruiting notable BOD members
- Developing a go to market strategy
- Developing a business model and supporting metrics
- Handling the legal aspects of startup formation
- Scaling a team and establishing employee compensation plans

2. Previous Exits

A founder with direct experience selling a startup or merging it with another company is incredibly valuable to a new founding team. A founder with exit experience is likely to have the skills needed to help the new venture reach critical milestones like securing funding, landing early customers, and founding a solid advisory board.

Previous exit experience usually comes in two key forms. Either the person was a founder who led the startup or, the person was a member of the startup leadership team (for example, VP of Technology, CFO, or another leadership role). Additional tools a founder may have developed during a prior exit include experiences in:

- Finding and engaging with potential acquisition partners
- Understanding the nuances of asset-based acquisitions verses equity-based acquisitions
- Managing team transitions and employee retention issues
- Hiring and working with M&A consultants

- Following and understanding the legal processes related to acquisitions

3. Domain Expertise

Founders with extensive experience in a specific industry, for example the credit card processing industry, are said to have deep *domain knowledge*. These founders have worked at, or built, companies that play a major role in a particular field or industry.

They know industry specific information, such as who the key players are, what weaknesses exist in current competitive offerings, how the technical implementations work, and what opportunities to improve or reshape the offerings in the industry segment are available. For a new startup attempting to disrupt a well established industry such as card processing, having a co-founder who really knows the industry on the team is worth giving that expert some additional equity.

Additional examples of domain expertise include a deep understanding of:

- Industry and market interconnections and inner workings
- The trends and influencing forces shaping the market
- Regulatory, environmental, and political influences.
- Both the historical technology and new advances in the industry

4. Technical Expertise

Founders with extensive technical expertise might also warrant more equity. Skills as diverse as coding, working with cloud services such as Amazon Web Services (AWS), database schema development, hardware engineering, industrial design, and hiring a technical team all make the technical expertise list. Additional examples include:

- Minimum viable product (MVP) development, testing, and enhancement
- Technical team recruiting, scaling, and management
- User interface design and user experience expertise

- Command of technical trends and industry players
- Product development tools and methodologies

5. Financial Expertise

Founders with exceptional financial expertise can accelerate a startup to new levels of success. A founder with this type of exceptional skill brings more than just basic accounting or book keeping skills to the table. Rather, he or she brings experience with building financial models and cash flow projections, and understanding how key decisions impact the balance sheet. Additional qualifications of exceptional financial expertise include:

- Deep understanding of the core financial statements—income statement (P&L), balance sheet, cash flow, and so on
- Ability to perform financial modeling of the startup's business and revenue projections
- Ability to manage startup equity decisions and the capitalization (cap) table
- Banking and lending relationships and expertise
- Knowledge of startup tax rules and regulations
- Ability to implement accounting and controlling checks and balances

6. Customer Development Expertise

The cornerstone of every successful startup is providing elegant solutions to very well defined customer segments. Startup founders must identify who the company's customers are, what pain points the startup's solution really fixes for them, and how well the startup's product or service fits with the market compared to other solutions. Founders with customer development experience know that getting out of the office to meet with early customers is key to discovering what potential customers will buy. (For more detailed thoughts on this, see the excellent book on the customer discovery and development process by Steve Blank and Bob Dorf, *The Startup Owner's Manual: The Step-by-Step Guide for Building a Great Company*.) This category includes more detailed expertise in:

- Arranging customer meetings with detailed interviews and product fit discussions
- Knowing how customers use competing products including likes and dislikes
- Identifying how your customers want to interact with you and your team and your product
- Collaborating with customer teams to refine or reject your product or solution.
- Iterating MVP development cycles, driven by customer feedback
- Defining go or no-go decision milestones

7. Sales Expertise

Dig into the heart of a successful startup, and you will find a sustained and predictable sales process. Whether your company is selling your product or service to direct to end users by tweaking your online engagement flow or selling to other businesses, a founder who knows how to engage your company's ideal customers is one of the keys that unlocks early proof that your market cares about your product.

Additional demonstrated sales mastery includes experiences in:

- Developing the sales process, including providing a clear view of the sales cycle
- Developing and managing the sales pipeline
- Building a sales team and compensation structure
- Building channel partner relationships
- Establishing early adopter agreements with notable customers
- Identifying and nurturing customer champions that will give testimonials and recommendations
- Articulating the sales landscape—end customers, technical buyers, economic buyers, and so on
- Identifying and understanding competitors, including strengths, weaknesses, and key leadership

8. Marketing Expertise

Marketing can be summarized as creating a message about your company and products and conveying it to your ideal customers, the media, and other stakeholders. Founders with great marketing skills know how to develop a story around the startup and its products, and create awareness, curiosity, understanding, and ultimately, action by a prospective customer who digs deeper into your solution. Additional skills in the marketing category include:

- Developing and testing marketing campaigns
- Building repeatable marketing processes with associated metrics
- Maximizing social media marketing opportunities
- Developing and managing a marketing calendar
- Building marketing tools for the sales team
- Creating and maintaining a world class PR presence

9. Fundraising Expertise

Founders with fundraising expertise know how to raise money to fund the startup's growth. They know what angel and VC investors want and how the startup equity fundraising process works. If you are building a high-growth startup that requires large cash injections to reach key milestones, a founder who has successfully raised equity funding is invaluable. Additional fundraising expertise includes understanding:

- What stage your startup must be at to attract equity investors
- State and federal securities regulations related to early-stage investing
- Investor courting, pitching, and due diligence
- Equity deal structures—straight equity, convertible debt, equity crowdfunding
- Cap table development and management
- Funding roadmap development with funding needs and uses

- Startup valuation methods and implications
- Financial and equity impact of investor term sheet deal points

Be Careful with Big Titles

Big titles such as CEO or CTO can pigeonhole founders into specific roles, with negative side effects.

Many savvy startup founders choose to leave titles out of their organization during the very early stages of their new venture, choosing instead to call everyone simply a co-founder. Without lofty titles, you reduce the risk that somebody claims that a task is not fitting for their title: "Clean the toilets, Steve! I don't care if you are CEO." When your startup reaches a more mature stage with more employees and managers, then you can assign titles and grant each person the appropriate authority of a particular position.

Using The Equity Split Scorecard

With these nine "startup success factors" in mind, let's walk through the steps your team can follow to determine if you or your co-founders have the exceptional skills that warrant additional equity.

1. ***Score each founder on the success factors.*** Each founder should rate him-or herself using a copy of the 2a. Rate Yourself tab of the Equity Split Workbook file. Just type a 1 into the cell for the rating percentage to assign for each of the nine Gold Star Factors listed. To receive a Gold Star, the founder must score in the 130% range or better.

In the example graphic below, Founder Bob has previous startup experience and previous exit experience, having sold his startup for a large win. Compared to the average startup founder in the startup world, this is significant experience. Bob gets a Gold Star in the 1. Startup Leadership Expertise and 2. Previous Exit Expertise rows.

The Equity Split Scorecard: Rate Yourself										
Founder Name: Bob										
							Gold Star Earned... →			
Gold Star Factor	70%	80%	90%	100%	110%	120%	130%	140%	150%	Gold Star
1. Startup Leadership Expertise								1		✪
2. Previous Exit Expertise							1			✪
3. Domain Expertise				1						
4. Technical Expertise				1						
5. Financial Expertise					1					
6. Customer Development Expertise			1							
7. Sales Expertise			1							
8. Marketing Expertise			1							
9. Fundraising Expertise					1					

Typical Founder   Exceptional Founder

2. **Enter the Bonus Equity Percentage to set the size of the bonus equity pool.** After each founder has scored his/herself using the 2a. Rate Yourself tab, next move to the 2b. The Equity Split Scorecard tab and enter the total amount of bonus equity that will be awarded to founders with significant skills in the cell to the right of the Bonus Equity Percentage label. In our example, the three founders decided to enter 25% as the Bonus Equity Percentage.

Bonus Equity Percentage:	25%

The bonus equity will be divided via the rest of this process, with some founders giving up some equity percentage points to the other founder(s)—a reward for notably advantageous skills and experience that will accelerate the startup toward success.

3. *Enter the names of each founder in the Founder Name row.* Enter the names of each founder, which will appear in blue as shown below. The formulas in the Everybody Starts Equal row will calculate an equal ownership in the startup, 33.33% per founder in our example. At the end of scoring each founder, the Bonus Equity Percentage entry will be divided up and added as applicable to each founder's starting equity, resulting in the total amount of equity allocated to each founder. Note that if your team has four founders, there is an additional column available for a fourth founder's name (to the right of Jill in the example.)

Founder Name:	Bob	Steve	Jill		
Everybody Starts Equal:	33.33%	33.33%	33.33%		100%
Equity Less the Bonus Pool:	25.00%	25.00%	25.00%	0.00%	

4. *Enter each Founder's Gold Stars into The Equity Split Scorecard.*

Next, continuing down the scorecard to the Gold Star Score section, enter a 1 for each factor for which the founder scored a gold star on his or her copy of the 2a. Rate Yourself tab. In our example here, Founder Bob earned a gold star for 1. Startup Leadership Experience and one for 2. Previous Exit Expertise, so he gets a 1 entered for each factor. And Founder Jill earned a gold star for being exceptional in the 4. Technical Expertise category. As you see, these gold stars result in allocating 67% of the Bonus Equity Percentage to Bob and 33% to Jill.

Gold Star Score					
Startup Success Factors	Bob	Steve	Jill		
1. Startup Leadership Experience	1	0	0	0	
2. Previous Exit Expertise	1	0	0	0	
3. Domain Expertise	0	0	0	0	
4. Technical Expertise	0	0	1	0	
5. Financial Expertise	0	0	0	0	
6. Customer Development Expertise	0	0	0	0	
7. Sales Expertise	0	0	0	0	
8. Marketing Expertise	0	0	0	0	
9. Fundraising Expertise	0	0	0	0	
Other					
Other					
Other					
Other					
Total Gold Stars	2	0	1	0	3
Resulting Bonus Equity %	67%	0%	33%	0%	100%

5. *Review the resulting division of the Bonus Equity Percentage.* The Amount of Bonus Equity Earned row calculates how much each founder gets of the Bonus Equity. Percentage In our example, Bob gets 16.7% of the bonus equity, Jill gets 8.3%, and Steve does not receive any additional equity. The Final Equity split row adds each founder's initial equity from the Everybody Starts Equal row with the amount calculated in the Amount of Bonus Equity Earned row. In the example, the calculated suggested equity split 41.67% for Bob, 25% for Steve, and 33.33% for Jill.

Amount of Bonus Equity Earned:	16.7%	0.0%	8.3%	0.0%	
Final Equity Split:	41.67%	25.00%	33.33%	0.00%	100%

Add or Substitute Success Factors

Feel free to substitute or add success factors to the lists on the 2a. and 2b. tabs as needed to customize the worksheets as needed.

For example, consider a founder worked for several years on R&D and getting a patent on the core technology that is the foundation of the startup's core product line. In this case, the founder's exceptional expertise and work completed on the foundational technology of the startup warrants some additional equity.

In this case, you could add a Patent/IP success factor to the tabs and give the founder a gold star.

Back to Equal Equity Splits

What happens if no one is exceptional in any of the success factors listed on the 2a. Rate Yourself tab? If none of the founders earns a Gold Star for notable skills or expertise, or everybody ended up with an equal number of gold stars, you can just use tab 2b. The Equity Split Scorecard as a tool to divide up the bonus equity equally by skipping the Bonus Equity Percentage entry and entering the founder names. This is OK and is a clear indication that dividing the equity ownership into equal parts is a good solution for your startup.

In summary, using The Equity Split Scorecard process provides a simple structure for you and your co-founders to talk about "who is really great at what." At the end of the process, you can be confident that you have talked openly about each of your strengths and weaknesses, and awarded more equity to the co-founders on your team that truly have exceptional skills.

4

Vesting: Earning Your Piece of the Pie

As we learned earlier in this guide, one of the three rules of founder equity splits is that **everybody must vest**. With Step 1 (the Founder Test), and Step 2 (agreeing on the founder equity splits) complete, you are now ready for Step 3—creating vesting schedules for each founder.

You can think of the equity split question as how much ownership is fair for each founder, and vesting as "earning" that fair share by way of your work and commitment.

To get started, lets review the basics of startup vesting.

Vesting 101

In plain English, *vesting* means that you don't actually own you stock shares until certain events or timeframes have occurred. For example, a common startup vesting schedule results in each founder "earning" 25% of his or her ownership at the person's one-year anniversary with the company. In other words, you have to stay with the startup effort for at least one year to get 25% of your equity. For example, if your equity split is 50/50, a founder with 25% vested ownership owns 12.5% of the overall company (25% of 50% = 12.5%, right).

Vesting helps keep everybody working hard, even through the difficult times. If everybody has to stick with the startup to earn their founder shares according to a vesting schedule, there is more incentive to tough out he hard spots. In contrast, if each founder gets his or her full equity granted from day one, then there is less incentive to stick with the startup when the going gets tough.

A Super Important Point on Vesting

With vesting, you are not answering the question "How much equity do I get?", but rather, "how do I earn the equity we've already agreed that I own?"

Put another way, vesting does not change the equity percentages split you arrived at using The Equity Split Scorecard, but rather provides a framework to earn your equity according to the vesting rules you agree to with your co-founders.

Vesting Solves Potential Issues

There are a number of situations where one founder is not able to put the amount of work that he or she agreed to handle. Startup founders are always juggling the realities of life. For example, the vesting schedule comes into play to help resolve equity questions in situations like these:

- **Founder Leaving.** Vesting offers a framework to minimize the equity impact of a Founder leaving the startup effort. If a founder leaves, any unvested equity reverts to the company for use in recruiting replacement talent.

- **Part-Time Founder.** Vesting provides a mechanism for part-time founders to earn equity over time as they complete their portion of the startup's tasks. See "The Part-Time Founder" section for more details about part time founder vesting.

- **A Founder Not Performing Well.** Vesting offers a mechanism to reduce the equity impact of a poorly performing founder. Perhaps he or she has lost interest, has found the challenge of working for a startup is proving too difficult, or has other life priorities getting in the way. Either way, the founder is not able to contribute at the agreed-upon level.

- **Personal Situations such as Illness, Divorce, or Death of Someone Close.** Any of these situations can cause a well intending and committed founder to simply not be able to put in enough time and attention for an extended period of time. Vesting provides a mechanism to account for these common occurrences.

Vesting Terminology

Before moving on to learning about some common startup vesting structures, let's quickly review the common terms founders will encounter when discussing equity and vesting.

Time-Based Vesting. This type of vesting means that the vesting schedule is tied to the calendar. With time-based vesting, founders earn their equity by showing up and working on the startup effort over a period of months and years. For example, the founders might agree to a standard 4-year vesting schedule—a 4 year period in total, with 25% each founder's shares vesting at the end of 1 year, and then 1/48th of the remaining shares will vest each month until the end of the 4 year period. Time-based vesting is the most common vesting structure.

Milestone-Based Vesting. With milestone-based vesting, founders must achieve agreed-upon milestones to earn portions of founder equity. For example, founders might agree that when the startup launches its beta product with 10 early customers, the founders will each earn 20% of his or her founder's equity. Unlike time-based vesting, this method is not about time passing on the calendar, but rather achieving critical tasks needed to move the startup forward.

Vesting Acceleration. With this method, an event takes place that causes a change in the vesting schedule of founder shares. For example, if another company acquires the startup, the founder's agreement might state that each founder's stock vesting will accelerate to 100% vested. Vesting acceleration is further defined to two additional terms:

Single Trigger. Also referred to as "acceleration on change of control," with a single trigger, a founder's equity ownership accelerates to 100% vested if the startup is acquired.

51

Double Trigger. A "double trigger" requires two events for acceleration to occur: 1. Your startup gets acquired and 2. your role changes significantly, such as being terminated by the acquiring company. It makes sense that founders should be protected by acceleration clauses tied to their vesting schedules.

Cliff. A cliff is startup lingo for the waiting period before a founder gets any equity vested. Put another way, a vesting cliff is a time-based milestone that must be crossed before a specific percentage of your equity ownership vests. As we learned earlier, the common vesting percentage and cliff duration is 25% at one year, meaning that you have to stay with the startup for one year at which point you then get 25% of your founder's equity.

Founder Vesting Schedules

Vesting can be time-based or milestone-based. The following sections review each of these vesting mechanisms in more detail.

Time-Based Vesting

Vesting schedules for founders' shares can vary. Founders can choose to have a percentage of their equity vest each year, or each quarter.

The most common time-based vesting schedule follows this schedule: **the equity vests over four years, with a one year cliff for the first 25%, and each additional 1/48th of the shares vesting each month thereafter for the next three years.** Recall that the "cliff" terminology means that the shareholder has to wait the duration of the cliff period, a full year (in this example) before he or she earns any equity. This schedule provides a hefty incentive for the founder to get things done and stay the course.

The following graphic shows the standard startup vesting schedule.

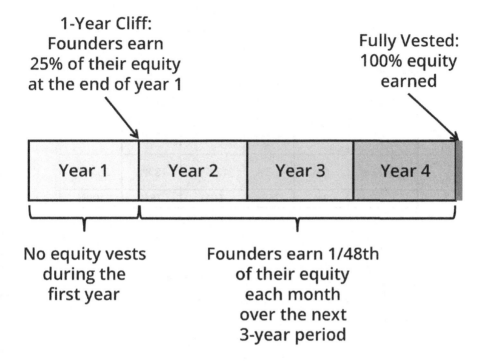

Standard Startup Vesting

1-Year Cliff:
Founders earn 25% of their equity at the end of year 1

Fully Vested: 100% equity earned

| Year 1 | Year 2 | Year 3 | Year 4 |

No equity vests during the first year

Founders earn 1/48th of their equity each month over the next 3-year period

Revisiting our three example founders and their equity split agreement, the graphic below shows how the equity vesting plays out for Bob, Jill, and Steve, using the standard 4-year vesting with a 1-year cliff for 25%.

	Equity Split Agreement	Year 1	25%	Year 2	Year 3	Year 4
Founder Bob	41.67%	0%	10.4%	20.8%	31.3%	41.67%
Founder Jill	33.33%	0%	8.3%	16.7%	25.0%	33.33%
Founder Steve	25.00%	0%	6.3%	12.5%	18.8%	25.00%
Total	100%	0%	25%	50%	75%	100%

1-Year Cliff: Founders earn 25% of their equity at the end of year 1

1/48th earned each month over the next 3-year period

Fully Vested: 100% equity earned

Unequal Vesting Schedules

Vesting schedules for each founder do not have to equal. For example, the founding team of three may agree that since one of the founders has completed significant work before the other founders joined the startup effort, 25% of the lead founder shares would vest immediately, while the newly joining founders would have to wait a year before 25% of their shares vest.

Milestone-Based Vesting

As you learned in the previous section, time-based vesting is common. That said, just having time pass does not guarantee that founders show up, charge ahead, and get things done. This is not to say that it's a common tendency for startup founders to slack off, but there are always life circumstances that get in the way of best intentions.

Milestone-based vesting accounts for work done, not time that has passed. In other words, founders earn some of their equity by checking tasks off the startup's to-do list.

With milestone-based vesting, you and your founding team agree on key milestones, that when reached, trigger X% of founder equity to vest.

Establishing a milestone-based vesting schedule keeps founders laser focused on the most important aspect of any startup—getting a working version of the company's product or service in front of paying customers.

Milestone vesting is also especially good to help solve equity questions related to part-time founders. Refer to the section titled "The Part-Time Founder" for more details.

Individual Milestones

In this twist on milestone-based investing, establishing milestones customized for each founder gives each founder motivation to complete specific tasks that fall under his or her role in the startup. For example, the business-talented founder might hit a vesting milestone when he completes the business plan, executive summary, and supporting financials. Or, the technically talented founder hits her vesting milestone when she completes the public beta testing of the company's new app.

Collective Milestones

In contrast to establishing individual milestones, with collective milestone vesting, all founders vest a certain amount of equity when the startup as a whole achieves an important milestone. Such as, "we all agree that 10% of our equity will vest upon the successful funding of $100,000 or more."

The following list provides several example startup milestones that could be used as vesting milestones:

- Launching the low-fidelity minimum-viable product (MVP)
- Launching the high fidelity MVP
- Closing a critical industry partnership deal
- Reaching a revenue target
- Closing on a funding goal
- Signing 100, 500, or 1,000 users

- Completing a regional product roll out
- Fully documenting the startup's operating procedures
- Coding an MVP
- Raising investment capital
- Designing and launching the website
- Executing marketing tasks
- Developing a new product
- Completing a measurable and repeatable marketing campaign
- Establishing the core metrics for the business

Combining Time-Based and Milestone-Based Vesting

Founders can choose to combine time-based vesting with milestone-based vesting.

Let's look at how our example founders might combine these two types of vesting and apply it to their equity split agreement.

Recall that in our earlier example, our team used The Equity Split Scorecard to arrive at the following equity split: Bob gets 41.67%, Steve gets 25%, and Jill gets 33.33%.

The group decides to use a mixed vesting plan, using milestone-based vesting for the first 25% of equity, and then switching to a standard time-based vesting plan for the remaining 75%.

The founders spent a day together mapping out the key milestones that will trigger the first 25% equity vesting. Here are the milestones they chose.

Technical. Completing the MVP of their SaaS tools for the credit card processing industry.

Customer Development. Securing 25 beta customers to test the MVP with, and collect feedback.

Funding. Complete pitch decks, executive summary, and supporting financial projections to present to potential investors and supporters.

Once the team hits these key milestones, they will switch to the standard time-based vesting where 1/48th of each founder's equity vests each month over the next three-year period.

The mixed vesting plan allows the founders to earn a chunk of equity quickly, if they all hit the milestones. If they hit the milestones in 5 months, they earn 25% of their equity. In contrast to a standard time-based vesting plan, they would have to wait an entire year to earn the 25%.

Documenting Vesting Progress

Once everybody's vesting clock has started ticking, it's a good idea to schedule short meetings every calendar quarter to document time-based vesting.

Documenting milestone-based vesting progress is equally important. When a significant vesting milestone has been completed, it's a good idea to have a quick founder meeting where all founders can agree that the milestone has truly been achieved. Keep a simple spreadsheet to track each founder's vesting progress, as well as a backup somewhere in the cloud or as a dated hard copy.

Some milestones are very clear—a signed deal with a major customer, for example. Either the deal is signed, or it's not. Signing up your first 100 users is another clear milestone.

Completing other milestones can be less clear, such as completing a MVP for a web service platform. In this example, software development is rarely ever "done." There are always minor bugs to fix, designs to be improved, user flows to be tested, and so on. In this type of case, the vesting milestone would be better worded as "Launching our MVP with 25 users." With this wording, either you've launched with 25 users or not. The details and small changes to the MVP remain on the to-do list, but for the purposes of vesting, the milestone has been completed.

If more work is needed on a vesting milestone, then all founders should agree to what "checked off the list" looks like, and everybody should go back to work to make it happen.

5

Common Equity Split Questions

The following sections review several common equity split questions founders frequently encounter, including:

- It was my idea, shouldn't I get more equity?
- I can invest a big chunk of money in the startup. How much equity should I own compared to my co-founders?
- I have the great idea for a startup, but I need a software developer to architect and code the product. How much equity should I give my developer friend?
- I'm a solo founder and have completed two years of work on the startup. I'm now recruiting two co-founders to help build the startup. How much equity should I give the folks who are late to the game?

The Big Idea

Problem. I came up with the idea and told my co-founders about it. We collectively decided to start the new venture, but shouldn't I get more equity because it was my idea?

Solution 1. Simply, no. Most experienced entrepreneurs will argue that ideas have little or no value. The value in the startup is created by validating the idea in the marketplace—completing tasks on the to-do list, building the product, selling it to customers that truly care about your solution to their problem. It will take the full effort of all the founders involved to make the startup a success. And all the founders need to be rewarded for their effort and commitment by owning a significant piece of the pie.

Therefore, you don't get to have more of the equity just because it was your idea.

Tossing the idea guy a few extra percentage points might seem like a non-issue in term of overall ownership, but it rewards the wrong thing.

Solution 2. Use The Equity Split Scorecard for ideas born from deep domain expertise. If the founder with "the idea" also has exceptional experience in the field of the startup's target market, then perhaps he or she deserves an additional chunk of equity.

Deep domain expertise often leads to an idea to center a startup on. Say Founder Bob worked for many years in the financial services industry and realized that a certain customer segment has a serious pain point. Founder Bob devises a solution (the idea) to solve this customer pain, and moves ahead with two co-founders to build a business. Founder Bob has significant insider knowledge of the financial services industry, lots of customer contacts, and connections with other players that can lead to great business partnership opportunities. In this case, Founder Bob has deep domain expertise, perhaps enough to warrant some additional points of equity.

Circle back to the The Equity Split Scorecard section to evaluate the idea-guy's level of skills and expertise.

The Founder-Investor

Problem: One founder is able to put a large sum of cash into the startup to get the startup off to a great start. Shouldn't this founder be entitled to more of the founder equity pie?

Solution 1. Create a bootstrap fund first.

First, make sure you really need the additional founder money.

Before tackling the sticky issue of a founder-investor, many founders choose to create a bootstrap fund. The bootstrap fund enables the startup team to delay the need for bigger funding from the founders themselves or from outside sources like friends and family supporters, angels and VC investors, or crowdfunding options.

Each founder puts in an equal amount of cash to get the startup off of square one. For example, three founders might each put in $5,000 for a total of $15,000. They previously created a initial formation budget and think the bootstrap fund will cover the initial costs of common items like a basic website, early product development, travel costs for visiting early customers, and so on.

If the startup needs significant capital beyond the bootstrap fund and one of the founders has the financial resources to inject a big chunk, then evaluate the following solution.

Solution 2: Treat the founder money like an outside investment round. Make your founder equity split decision first, then choose an investment structure for the founder's big money injection. At this point, the founder is both a founder and an investor, or a founder-investor, if you will.

A few possible structures to apply to the founder-investor's cash injection include convertible debt, straight equity (either common shares or preferred shares), or a simple loan.

Equity for Code (or Other Services)

Problem. Using equity to pay a contractor for services. In this example, the startup has very little cash to hire a developer, so the founders offer the developer a piece of the equity ownership pie. Handing out small bits of equity to service providers is a common temptation—1% to a great designer for a logo and brand look and feel, .5% to an trusted advisor, or 5% to a developer all seem like small enough amounts to not really matter in the long run. After all, early-stage startups are cash poor, so why not user equity to get some thing done?

Two problems typically emerge trading equity for code (or other services).

1. You are likely to change developers. It's a gamble to find a developer who will hit the mark the first time. Say you have handed out 5%, to the developer, the person kind of met the challenge, but you're not 100% satisfied. The developer loses interest, and you have to find a new developer. The 5% you've given to the first developer has become dead weight equity. If you

are still cash poor at this point, do you dole out another 5% equity and run the risk of a second service provider walking away with some of your limited equity in hand?

2. You will always need engineers. If you are a technology startup (apps, web services, SaaS, and so on), you are always going to need skilled engineering talent. Are you going to give up more equity to get the next stage of development completed every step of the way?

Solution 1. Recruit a talented co-founder to fill the needed role, such as developer. Finding a co-founder who believes in the vision of the startup and is willing and able to join with co-founder status (be sure the new founder passes The Founder Test) solves the technical gap issue. While, yes, you are indeed trading equity for the development services of the skilled co-founder, but the skilled co-founder is joining the team for the long haul. Finding a talented co-founder is often very difficult and fraught with pitfalls and complications. But if you find a great person with the right chemistry, the value to the startup will be the difference between success and failure.

Solution 2. Use stock options to pay the developer. Some startups choose stock options as a currency to pay service providers such as software or hardware engineers or development companies. The startup carves out a portion of equity of the company in the form of stock options, say 20% for example. If the service provider agrees to this form of compensation, the startup grants stock options for value of the work completed. The service provider then has the option to buy the startup's stock at a certain price, within a defined timeframe. The idea is as the startup grows, its valuation increases and the value of its stock also increases. If the startup is lucky and gets acquired, the option holders are likely to get a cash return for the shares they own.

If you choose to take the path of issuing stock options in exchange for development work, be aware there are securities laws regulating the use of equity (stock) for compensating both employees and other service providers. There are also important tax implications for both the startup and the contractor, such as whether stock options are granted as an Incentive Stock Options (ISO) or Non-incentive Stock Options (NSO).

Work with your startup lawyer and CPA to help you navigate these complex rules and regulations.

Solution 3. Set up a revenue sharing plan. With a revenue sharing payment model, the contractor gets paid a specified percentage of the revenue each month. Unlike a standard bank loan requiring that a set amount has to paid each month, revenue sharing flows and ebbs with the startup's revenue ups and downs.

For example, let's say the startup and software developer agrees to a value of $10,000 for the development work that needs to be done. Once the developer delivers the software according the specs, the startup pays the contractor 5% of the topline revenue, once the software has been released and there are paying customers, of course.

As a sweetener to offset the risk and to account for the delay between when the work is completed and the startup getting paying customers, the startup might also agree to pay the contractor up to two time (2X) the value of the development work, or $20,000.

If the startup's revenues are decent, say $30,000 per month, the contractor would receive a payment of $1,500 per month (0.05 x $30,000 = $1,500). If the revenues continue at this pace, it will take 14 months to pay the contractor the agreed 2X amount ($20,000).

While it may take the startup longer to reach the total payment amount (as compared to a lump sum payment), the contractor is getting a payment that coincides with the startup's revenues. And the contractor doesn't take the same risk as an equity investor that is betting on an all-or-none outcome for his or her investment.

Of course, the contractor takes a risk that the startup might fail to generate revenue, therefore this model is best suited for startups that are on track to predictable revenue. Startups that don't have a revenue model in place, such as Internet plays seeking to gain users rather than revenue, obviously don't fit this model.

Pro Tip

IP and Contractor Work for Hire Agreements

Make sure outside contractors such as software developers, designers, or anyone doing work for the startup assigns all intellectual property (IP) or code created by the contractor to the startup using a simple "Work for Hire" agreement. The Work for Hire agreement makes it very clear that this startup owns all of the IP associated with the contractor work, and the contractor has no claim on the work or its value to the startup.

Work Already Completed by a Solo Founder

Problem: If one founder has already worked for many months independently on R&D, market validation, and other key product tasks, shouldn't she be entitled to a large share of the startup equity? After all, without her effort, there would be no product to build the startup around.

After validating her product is compelling to a few early customers, the early work founder recruits two new co-founders to round out the startup team and help launch the startup. Is this hard working innovator entitled to more equity than her new co-founders?

Solution: Vest the early work founder equity faster. Instead of allocating more equity to the initial founder (that could feel unfair to the highly skilled new founders), consider setting up a vesting schedule where the early work founder earns a portion of the agreed upon equity split faster, in proportion to the amount of work already done. Remember, the goal is to maintain a high level of incentive for all founders. It's a long, hard road ahead, and everyone on the team needs to feel fairly compensated for the risks they are taking.

Let's say Founder Jill worked for a full year developing the code and algorithms for a new search engine.

Jill then recruits Steve and Bob as co-founders to help build a business around this software. They have agreed to equal equity splits of 33.33% each, with a standard vesting schedule (25% shares at the end of year 1, and 1/48th each month until the end of year four.) Because Jill has already put in a huge amount of work over the course of the last year, Steve and Bob agree that hard working Jill deserves to have 25% of her shares vest immediately. Steve and Bob will have to wait until their one-year anniversary for their 25% vesting to occur.

The Part Time Founder?

Problem. One of our co-founders can only work part-time on the startup effort. How do we handle the equity split decision?

There are a number of reasons a founder might not be able to work on the startup effort full-time, some good, others not so good.

Good Reasons To Justify Being a Part-Time Founder

I'm extending my personal runway. Personal cash flow needs often dictate the timing of joining a startup effort on a full-time basis. Common circumstances include:

- Completing a current consulting contract to pack away more savings that can be tapped later when enduring a lean startup paycheck

- Needing to wait until partner or spouse gets a job. Maintaining a support system at home is the basis for many founders having the freedom to work on a startup effort full time

I'm completing previous commitments. Many startup founders fully intend to join the startup effort on a full time-basis, but need to finish up other obligations. Examples include:

- Waiting for non-compete with a previous employer to expire
- Waiting until the semester is over and or until graduation occurs.

I'm Not Sure About You Guys, Yet.

Newly acquainted founders might not be sure about other founding team members, wanting to "date" before getting "married." If there are uncertainties about the team makeup, consider establishing a three-month probation period for everyone. During the probation period, everybody works together on early startup tasks, giving the new partners time to learn the quirks and habits the earlier co-founders. If at the end of the three months everybody is still excited and ready to commit to each other, then move ahead with your equity split decision and the other task needed to move the startup onward.

Bad Reasons to Justify Being a Part-Time Founder

I'm waiting to see "if it works." The "if it works" attitude is a big red flag and signals a clear lack of commitment by the uncertain founder. A founder who intends to let everyone else do the work to reach key validations in the startup's roadmap should be avoided. Disinvite this part-time founder from the equity discussion as soon as possible.

I'll join when you get funded. Needing to get a paycheck is a legitimate concern for all of us working stiffs. The part-time founder who has to keep his or her day job until the startup raises enough money to provide a steady paycheck should really be considered an early employee, not a founder. He or she is not taking the same risk as other founders who work without a predictable paycheck.

If all the founders are keeping day jobs and working part time on the startup effort, then it's a different story. Use time-based vesting to protect the full-time founders (full-timers vest faster), and use milestone-based vesting to provide part-time founders an incentive to accomplish tasks on the startup's to-do list.

Suggested Ground Rules for Part-Time Founders

1. **Agree to go full time.** Establish agreement that the part-time founder can only get founder status if the intent is to go full time at a later date. Without this basic agreement in place, the part-timer is something else—an advisor, a contractor, a mentor, or a service provider. These contributors can be compensated with other means—cash payments, IOUs, and in rare instances, stock options. But in the case of deciding your founder equity splits, don't make the mistake of including these roles in the founder equity equation. Part-time founders must have the intent of going full-time.

2. **List the conditions.** Create a short list of conditions that need to be for the part-timer to go full time. For example, Part-Time Founder Bob might need to complete his final semester at school prior to joining the startup on a full-time basis. Or, the part-time founder must complete a consulting obligation which ends in June. Once completed, the part-time founder will focus exclusively on the startup.

> **If you don't have a detailed plan to join the startup on a full-time basis, you are not a founder.**

3. **Establish a target timeline.** The part-timer should agree to a target timeline that shows when the part-timer can join the effort full time. Don't skip this step. Many conditions, such as graduation from school, might have obvious timelines, but others, such as the completing of a consulting engagement might not be so clear to all team members.

4. **Pass The Founder Test.** In other words, the part-time founder must fit into a full-time role in the startup. If the part-timer does not pass The Founder Test, then he or she is something else—a consultant, a contractor, an early employee.

5. **Use milestone-based vesting with fast-forwarding.** The part-time founder can "earn" equity by hitting agreed on milestones while working part time. But, the earned equity is considered truly vested until the part-timer goes full time, at which time, the earned equity "fast-forwards" and becomes the property of the founder.

The following figure shows how a part-time founder vesting schedule compares to a standard time-based vesting schedule. In this example, Founder Steve is working part-time developing the MVP for the startup. As agreed with Steve's co-founders, Bob and Jill, Steve will earn 25% of his equity split amount when they launch the MVP with 10 customers. And, when Steve joins the startup on a full-time basis in April, this earned 25% will vest. From there, Steve's remaining 75% equity will vest over a 3-year period. Compare this to Full time Founder Bob and Jill, who hit their 25% vesting at the end of year 1.

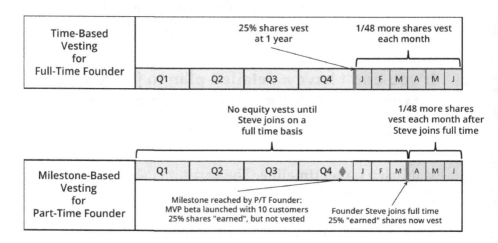

Making "being full time" a requirement for earning any equity might seem like an unforgiving rule. But consider the alternative. The part-time founder does some work but never joins the startup, yet is able to walk away with a piece of the ownership pie. The remaining founders would be left with huge gap in their team and would have to give up more of their equity to recruit a new founder to fill the gap. The dead weight founder stills owns a piece of the company but doesn't provide any ongoing value to the startup.

Too Many Founders?

How many is too many founders? Four, Five, Six? The best way to answer this question is to flip the question around. How few founders can we have and still be successful?

Like a car without an engine, or a plane without wings, you need enough founders to cover the critical areas of the startup. The car won't go if a major piece is missing, like the engine. The same is true for the startup founder mix. Get the mix right, with everybody's skills and experience filling the proper roles, and the chances of success are the highest. But get the mix wrong, with skills overlapping too much or by having too many founders trying to find their place, and then you're flirting with chaos.

Most experienced startup entrepreneurs and investors agree to the following:

- One founder is not enough

- Two is great

- Three is ok

- Four or more is asking for trouble

Remember, the question of part time verse full time is not so much about the hours spent, but most importantly, about milestones achieved. Part-time founders can make significant contributions to hitting big milestones, so don't cripple your chances of success by counting a skilled part-timer out of the startup equation.

6

Putting Your Equity Agreement In Writing

If you look back to our three rules of founder equity splits, the third rule says to **Set It and Forget It.** Meaning, once you've come to your equity split agreement with your cofounders, put the equity agreement and vesting schedules in writing, and then build your startup. This final section of our guide provides guidance on documenting your equity agreements.

Using a simple letter to document your agreement

For founders who have not completed all of the formal startup formation paperwork with their lawyer, documenting their equity split agreement can be as simple as a writing a one-page letter or email message. Be sure to have all the founders sign and date a hard copy of the letter, and make a copy of each of the signed documents for each founder.

You can keep it informal and efficient by using email, but be sure to have each founder confirm their agreement with an affirmative email response. Print hard copies of each message and response.

The following section offers an example of an equity split agreement letter.

Sample Equity Split Agreement Letter

Dear [Bob and Jill],

I'm writing to document our recent meeting where we came to a final agreement on the equity ownership of our new startup, [XYZ Corp].

During the meeting, we used the following method to arrive at an equity split agreement.

[pick one

- Equal splits, The Equity Split Scorecard, other method]

Our working file for the split work session and final results is [attached/ located here on our shared file storage].

The final agreement resulted in equity distribution as follows.

> *[Founder Bob: 33.33% equity*
>
> *Founder Steve: 33.33% equity*
>
> *Founder Jill: 33.33% equity]*

Additionally, we agreed to the following standard vesting schedule for our founder's shares:

[25% equity earned at the end of one year (1) from today's date, with 1/48th equity earned each month there after, until the end of year four (4).]

We agree that we will update our equity vesting once per quarter, and use the attached spreadsheet to document the vesting progress.

Finally, we agreed that this [letter/email] serves to document our equity agreement, until we take the steps to formalize all of our startup formation paperwork with a startup lawyer.

A hardcopy of this [letter/email] has been placed with our incorporation paperwork.

Please respond to the [letter/email] with your confirmation of the details herein.

Looking forward to an awesome startup journey with you guys,

Sincerely,

[Steve

Co-founder, XYZ Corp.]

After Incorporation and Other Formation Tasks

Documenting your founder equity split agreement takes on several additional layers when you get the lawyers involved (which you should).

It is quite common for founders to ignore the many startup formation tasks that lie beyond getting an LLC established with your state. They choose the company name, fill out the 1 or 2 page application and send it off to the state department of commerce, resulting the beginning stages of creating the legal corporate entity.

To get your startup housekeeping properly competed usually requires the help of an experienced startup lawyer. Law firms experienced in guiding startups through the maze of the legal documents and procedures will have a set of boilerplate agreements and templates that founders scan use to get started on these tasks. That said, be sure to read and understand these critical documents. Ask questions and clear up any confusion or item that are unclear.

Here is a list of the most common tasks and legal documents your startup lawyer will work with you to complete:

- Establish the number Authorized Shares for the corporation
- Establish a Par Value for the company's stock
- Issue Founder Shares
- Execute Founder's Stock Purchase Agreements
- Complete and file 83(b) Election paperwork
- Create an initial Cap Table for the startup
- Execute Invention Assignment, Non-compete, Non-disclosure agreements for each founder

While this seems like a long list, once you get these items out of the way, you don't have to revisit most of them for a long time. Events like taking on outside equity investors, such as Angel or VCs, trigger changes to many of these legal agreements.

Thank You!

This concludes the *Founder's Pocket Guide: Founder Equity Splits.* We hope you find our content and supporting tools useful for your startup journey.

We are always looking for feedback on our startup tools. If you have comments, feedback, or corrections, please send us a note.

info@1x1media.com

www.1x1media.com

###

Made in the USA
Las Vegas, NV
30 May 2024

90492012R00046